RANA ROO POETRY

AF059874

This edition first published in paperback by
Michael Terence Publishing in 2023
www.mtp.agency

Copyright © 2023 Rana Roo

Rana Roo has asserted the right to be identified as
the author of this work in accordance with the
Copyright, Designs and Patents Act 1988

ISBN 9781800945371

No part of this publication may be reproduced, stored
in a retrieval system, or transmitted, in any form or
by any means, electronic, mechanical, photocopying,
recording or otherwise, without the prior
permission of the publisher

Cover design
Copyright © 2023 Michael Terence Publishing

Contents

True Christmas 1
Thank You, Jesus 3
Hey Rana Roo 5
Never Give Up Hope 7
Passing the High School 9
Holy Mother 13
Gratitude 15
Don't Destroy 17
Life 19
Cheer 21
Seeds 23
Roo, My Love 27
Motherhood 29
Serving 31
Daily 33
18.5.2021 - Rana Roo 35
1982 - Fifteen 37
14.3.2015 - Don't Do It 41
1981 - My Best Friend 43
4.1.2011 - Mental Health 45
1987 - New Mum Soon 49

2020 - Coronavirus	51
1990 - Pregnancy	53
May 2021 - Smiling	55
Sorry Again	57
1979 - Class	61
Christian Music	63
May 2021 - Woods	65
Colour Red	67
Waking Up In May	69
It Won't Come To You	71
What I Do	75
Trust Yourself	77
Life	79
Written by My Eldest Granddaughter	81
Cliff Richard	83
Take The Good	85
Sarah	89
Memory Loss They Say	91
Remember To Walk Away	93
Grandchildren	95
Outside and Breathe	97
Each Day At A Time	99

True Christmas

The true meaning of Christmas,
It doesn't matter if the date of birth is wrong,
Jesus is here right now,
Hail Mary is so precious to pray,
Telling her everything I have to say,
Hail Mary Mother please show me,
Support me in learning more,
More than ever before,
Hail Mary Mother, oh holy one,
Thank you for the precious ability to pray to you,
May you talk to me as I sleep,
As I turn over on the bed in a heap,
May what you want me to know come into my mind and heart,
May you fill me up in my soul and every part,
Hail Mary, I am sorry I have failed you,
I am trying to listen,
Hail Mary precious Mother,
Thank you.

THANK YOU, JESUS

Lead us each day, when we open our eyes,
Faith is knowing how to help heal those cries,
Our needs are already known,
We may not always know why,
Those times are the mysteries,
The lock doesn't always fit the key,
Exotic fish in a fancy restaurant tank,
Dangerous oils enter our seas,
Married people try to connect elsewhere and tease,
Killings and false Gods looming in the air,
Evil around pretending they care,
Go where good is,
Don't follow the bad,
Give out happiness, don't make people sad,
The smallest of kindness,
Is not small at all,
Sprinkle it all wherever you go,
Help others to see,
Respecting each other and letting it be,
Christmas cards sent,
Gifts shared with loved ones,
Cooking that dinner,
Did you pass someone who needed a hand?
Was he cold in the corner,
Or in the queue at the stand?
Spotting a bargain for that person you know,
Pop it by their door without show,
That is how it all works,
Let's try today,
Loving you, me and all that you choose to see.

Hey Rana Roo,

Today my thoughts are totally with you,
We rescued a four-year-old spaniel you know?
I am not sure what you would have thought,
She was just waiting to be bought,
Her name is Dotty,
She lived in a garden you know?
So, the sofa and Hoover startled her at first,
Crikey, the little thing has a real thirst,
She doesn't like comfy dog beds,
In fact, they end up in tiny shreds,
I miss you, baby girl,
The pain does not heal,
All the what-ifs do not seem to go,
The walker, the car, me letting you go on the walk that day,
Not even able to say goodbye,
I hope you weren't in pain,
I nearly joined you, I couldn't take the strain,
You were not there to nudge me at three,
To come under the covers with me,
You no longer burped in my face,
Talked like a human,
You were a real classy case,
Stubborn and fussy and my best friend,
You're in my mind at every single bend,

Dotty needed rescuing,
You see she was not neutered and the man could not
    have her any more,
I love her and she is nothing like you,
It needed to be totally different you see,
Because you're always in me,
You have a proper grave now in my garden of flowers,
Jane cried you know,
She misses you too,
Karen came to see me and gave me a hug,
Becki and Adam came straight away,
They said I can do this and make another day,
I hope you are running in that dignified way of yours,
I hope you are playing and having some fun,
I hope the rainbow bridge is real,
I will see you one day,
I am sorry Rana Roo,
You're not here anymore to have your say,
Dotty, I share with Graham,
He came to say goodbye to you,
When we see a butterfly, we think it's you.

Never Give Up Hope

Wherever you are,
Whatever you have done,
Never give up hope,
Your journey takes on a new chapter now,
Your future is up to you,
You are the author of your life book,
When people put you down due to your past,
Simply say, "I don't live there anymore,"
Don't justify yourself,
Do your new thing,
Find friends who believe in you,
Not those who will watch you fall,
You can do this,
You can make that call,
An easy road, maybe not,
Some bumps to overcome,
Some words spoken that can't be undone,
Saying sorry to those who you can,
Make it right in their name if you can't,
Forgiving yourself and others will help you move forward,
Release yourself from the harm,
You'll soon see the opening for each wave to calm,
It really does not matter who you were then,
Each day is a new chance,
Each hour you can start again,
No judgement here,
Small steps are not to fear,
Climb them one at a time,
Embrace each day,

Everything will be just fine,
Remember you are never alone,
It takes courage to leave what you have known for so long,
I did it and still sometimes fail,
Work in progress is the trail,
Soon you'll see old habits have died,
New healthy ones taking place with pride,
You're here and I feel you,
It is going to be okay,
One hour at a time, day by day.

Passing the High School

Denes Academy, it says on the sign,
I pass it every day on the way to town,
Lots of students going in and out,
All seem polite, not one heard to shout,
Popping in for the Christmas fete,
Seeing teachers teaming with students and having fun,
Seeing lots of smiles and a joint effort in tow,
In the corridors, all walking slow,
Takes me back to my high school,
Not a good time for me,
This seems different, like a unity,
These students are our future,
Not to be dismissed at all,
They have opinions and thoughts and can make the call,
Education is a wonderful way for them to learn,
Equally, travel and listening to life's lessons as they go along,
Making the odd mistake and it's okay to get it wrong,
That's how we learn,
They need to know it's okay,
Mental health is important, not just reaching that grade,
Sometimes people with no grades still have it made,
Love and patience to hear them within,
Helping their beautiful journey begin,
Teaching respecting others and the earth they stand on,
Goes much further than some may think,
Life goes past in the blink of an eye,
A good feeling as I walk on by.

HOLY MOTHER

I am praying to you,
Sometimes I go straight through to the Lord,
Forgive me for not coming to you more often,
You are the Holy Hail Mary and there for me,
That in itself is a miracle, a wonder to be,
Hail Mary, as I get to know you,
As I learn about you and picture you back in that time,
May you have a special place in this heart of mine,
I was never taught the importance of you until now,
Miraculously, I went into that church as I walked by,
Three months later, learning a new journey for me,
Different aspects of the Bible leap out for me to see,
Friendly dedicated Priest and an elder gently show me what I ask,
Like a constant refilling of an empty flask,
Blessing the cross with Holy water as I went in,
Looking at your pictures all around me,
Beautiful love is what I see,
What you did for me,
Nothing short of a miracle and now I get to know more,
More than ever before,
Hail Mary Mother,
May I say help me when I am slipping?
Show me what to see,
I ask for your Holy blessing all over me.

Gratitude

Let us praise everything,
Little birds in the garden taking the seed,
Squirrels down the local park, taking from your hand a monkey nut,
Foot and plasters invented to go over a cut,
Staff in hospitals helping the unwell,
Priests in the church giving us God's word to tell,
Children on a train chatting and giggling away,
Some random people that pass you in the day,
Libraries that are still open and the staff within,
Greeting you with a smile and giving a helping hand,
Hot running water,
A nice cup of tea,
The world in your day, what you want it to be.

Don't Destroy

Passing the old town hall,
Standing there empty,
Beauty lies within,
Opportunities are all around,
Community projects to be found,
No idea, Lord,
You know what it could be used for,
Is there something I can do to save this beautiful old town hall?
Living here a year now,
Passing it every day,
Deteriorating the more it is left,
Makes me think of all the churches for sale,
No one seems to pay the bail,
Please do not demolish them,
Patience and prayer will show a way,
Please do not pop a block of flats on such sacred ground,
Another way can be found,
There is power in prayer,
Faith is to believe,
God always has something positive up his sleeve.

LIFE

Life has twists and turns,
It is okay not to be understood,
That's your own journey,
Not all will get,
Some will take an unfair bet,
Remember whose son or daughter you are,
Glance in that rear-view mirror and see how far you have come,
Those who put you down,
Are not your kind of people right now,
The right people will catch you up,
Believe and keep believing,
Your mind and heart will go on,
Straighten that crown and walk tall,
Plenty of us are here, having felt our call,
Yours is right there,
Just listen and hear,
Do not glance for long, do not fear,
You can do this, I know you can,
Jesus was sent down as a man,
To save you from your sins,
So that you will be totally okay,
your future is beautiful and strong,
In Him, we all help one another and belong.

CHEER

Christmas cheer,
Let's remember why we are here,
Ups and downs,
Turn the frown into the crown,
Pass the love to everyone you can,
Any living thing from a worm to a man,
Doing the serving completely in faith,
Smiling and being in that moment,
Showing how much we all care,
Making that difference everywhere,
I cannot reach your world,
You cannot reach mine,
Together we meet in middle, the love sign,
God's feeling in your tummy,
When you help another mummy,
Or you feed someone hungry,
When you rescue that dog who needs a home,
Sending the dogs homes blankets and a bone,
Volunteer in a care home,
Clean someone's home for free,
Feeling God's love is contagious you see.

Seeds

Seeds are showing love,
They are planted firmly in someone we choose,
We believe in them and know God will never refuse,
Watching them grow so full of fruit,
Compassion right from the root,
Gifts and money are not worth as much,
Praying for someone is the way,
Giving time to them on a set day,
You may be the only Bible some folk read,
You may be the only hope in someone's need,
Life, of course, requires money to pay bills,
Inner peace though does not come from
Inside through tills,
Your calling can be as simple as one, two and three,
Passing on God's love continuously.

Roo, My Love

Letting you go, my friend,
Is the hardest thing to do,
Knowing it was a horrible accident too,
Wanting to place some blame,
Never wanting to lose your name,
Whether the dog walker,
Or the car driver that hit you that day,
I want to be horrible,
I want to have my say,
The blame lies with me,
I let her take you, it should have been you and me,
I miss you more than you'll ever know,
You were never just a dog,
You were my best friend,
Helped me put life on the mend,
I wanted to follow you initially,
People didn't understand,
You and I faced the world together,
We joined in one hand,
Then I walked into church again,
Drew on my undeniable faith,
Gave Jesus all my tears and strain,
Tough is an understatement,
So hard still daily for sure,
Jesus for this pain is my only cure.

MOTHERHOOD

Refusing to talk to me,
I needed to step back,
The weight was too heavy in my sack,
Going your own way,
Doing your own thing,
I am attending church to pray and to sing,
Love has never changed,
There is no "but" in this love of mine,
Praying you're happy and you feel the shine,
I miss you Charlotte,
Mummy wants you to know,
If anything happens,
You carry on and grow,
Your children are adorable,
Each and every one,
Your work as a mummy never undone,
Seeing them all makes me smile,
I see you in them you know,
They have your beauty within and the outer glow,
Doing what is best for you, is the right thing to do,
I could not have carried on feeling the way I did,
You needed to explore the world and not be part of me,
Your journey is not for me to understand or see,
My love is unconditional and I am always here,
One day maybe we will walk again down Lowestoft pier,
My boundaries were part of my supporting you to be strong,
They were never about where you come from or belong,

Sometimes we all do what we feel is right,
Placing those guidelines down was the right thing to do for me,
Knowing one day in faith you will see,
Please be happy and healthy and look after yourself,
It is not about the world's possessions and wealth,
Praying for you every single day,
God's got a plan and purpose and I know He's on His way,
You're beautiful and kind,
With the most amazing mind,
I believe in you and most importantly, God does too.

SERVING

We are awake,
There is work to do,
Let's get serving, that is me and you,
Write something nice for the dear elderly man,
Do the shopping for a neighbour if you can,
It doesn't have to be a big serve,
This does not have to hit a bad nerve,
Everyone can do something small,
Even if it's helping to decorate a celebration hall,
Post a smiley face somewhere where it's clear,
Listen to someone's emotional fear,
We have it in us, it helps us to help them,
Whether children, women or men,
Doing someone's laundry, even if once,
Writing someone isolated a letter to read,
All help gel together a community need,
Do it gladly with a song in your heart,
Wake up asking, where do I start?

DAILY

Treetops blowing in the distance,
Children playing next door,
Wood being chopped for the fire,
Smelling the roses,
My heart is on fire,
What a change in me,
Only you could do this to me,
Thank you, Lord,
No more worry about my past,
Feeling sorry for myself is now last,
Making each day alive,
Being in the moment,
Squirrels running around,
Seed out for birds,
Water in their bowl,
Watching the mummy horse with her foal,
Appreciating everything,
Eyes open wide,
No longer feeling the need to hide,
Hail Mary, precious Mother,
You are so important to us all,
Teach me more,
Show me how to help in the fall,
I see the signs I didn't before,
On almost every door,
Some doors need closing,
Some doors stay ajar,
Some doors you run in from afar,
Thank you that I get it now,
For showing me your love,
Now I can pass it on to those who were blind,
That they can meet you in their heart and mind.

18.5.2021
RANA ROO

Gracefully built and powerful legs,
Sandy in colour,
Cute as can be,
Always in my heart to see,
Full of charismatic energy,
Fatigue days, what did we do?
Curl up in bed, I am in love with you,
Long walks and playing ball,
Digging holes and burying your bone,
Dirt all over your nose,
You never liked to be long alone,
Long fluffy ears upon your head,
You still think you're tiny as can be,
You're my inspiration, my reason to be me,
A year has gone by and now you are just gone two,
Noticing much more, and standing in sunsets and blue sky,
You have bought me alive again,
I will never be the same,
Let us enjoy our future together,
The divorce you saw me through,
Waking with that famous nudge to come under the covers,
You make everyone smile,
Let us learn together how to get through,
Just the future with me and you,
Interesting toys and a new friend,
You play with Rocky in the ocean,
Digging new dens,
I can never love an animal as I love you,
You're my special Rana Roo.

1982

Fifteen

Struggling I am to fit in this world,
I do not know what to do,
Diagnosed with Rheumatoid Arthritis,
Thanks for that, now what do I do?
The consultant says the future can be bleak,
Going upstairs, makes my legs feel weak,
School, I am being bullied,
To the teacher I won't name,
Stop hurling wooden rubbers at us,
Stop chalking a circle on the board for our noses to touch,
This is all getting too much,
Thank you to my English teacher, Mrs Davies your name,
For believing in me, write it all down you say,
You have a gift in a writing way,
I ran away to Surrey to Cliff Richard's home,
The police came and got me, I felt so alone,
Dad saying what is going on?
Yes, you are adopted but you really do belong,
I am sorry I keep letting you down,
My head is a mess I cannot work this out,
All I hear is a massive inner shout.

14.3.2015
DON'T DO IT

Breathing in and out,
I hear you are breaking the rules again,
I do hear you, I do,
I know you do not get life right now,
I was there also,
Taking slower breaths, to try and support us through,
Processing what is going on,
As another life begins to end,
Don't do it,
Don't break these particular rules,
Please do not go,
Please just go slow,
The cure can of course be found,
It is in how we react,
It is not about media facts,
Protecting a loved one is such a fight,
You are running wild out of sight,
I am left behind to pick up the pieces,
    I am not sure which way to go,
Don't do it please,
Stay local and do not run away,
Please do not go,
Do not leave me to be the one to always show,

Not sure what advice to give,
Only that God will always be your friend and forgive,
Worried about the not real you,
I know boundaries do not suit you,
You seem to want to explore,
You want more and more,
Responsibilities are here,
They should not be left to me,
I am tired too and tears roll down my face,
I see their faces and wash their teeth,
I see their hearts and all beneath,
It is in you, deep inside,
Please do not run, do not go and hide.

1981
MY BEST FRIEND

Rana Hennessey, you are my dear best friend,
Thank you for always calling around,
Thank you for looking past what others see,
Thank you for believing in me,
I am sorry I am not always in when you call for me,
I cannot face the world today so have gone to the beach,
I can face someone saying let me inside, you reach,
I am desperate to find me, I am desperate to see what you see,
One day in the adult world,
I will fall in love with an animal and call her your name,
If we should lose touch, she will be in honour of you,
I will tell her our stories, your loyalty,
How you inspire me,
I will call her Rana and how I feel will come alive all over again,
Just how much you mean to me,
Even if you may not always see,
I am sorry I was not always here,
I know you have lots to fear,
I see you, you know,
You little fighter,
When I am older, I will learn from you,
Right now, it is not in me, I need to run,
My head is a mess,
I do not know what to do,
Thank you for being my friend,
Although I am torn, you help me mend.

4.1.2011
Mental Health

Tears appear, and I do not know why,
Where did I go and why did I cry?
Those terrible wrongs I did, why?
How do I right them and move forward?
Where am I?
I feel trapped; the walls are closing in,
I need to escape but cannot,
Commitments and responsibilities,
I see them and feel them and can no longer run,
My brain cannot cope, I am hiding it all,
I wish someone somewhere would see the real me,
Hello, I am here, can you now see me?
I am falling inside, faking it on the out,
Tired not covering the feeling,
Knowing it could be worse does not cover it at all,
No one to help the real me if I fall,
Wisdom creeps in and that sucks even more,
Means I have to face everything,
Means I cannot run,
Hiding it by hanging with living on the edge,
Burying the pain,
Telling a lie,
Being a random inner spy,
How can I be loved, when I don't love myself?
I am scared,
Trapped emotions I put in the tin,
The walls are closer now, they are closing in,
Trying to please everyone and what about me?
I am sick of all this responsibility.

1987
NEW MUM SOON

My huge belly will soon deliver a boy or girl,
A son or daughter into this world,
Mum's reassurance with that disappointment
    I have split from their dad,
This makes me inner sad,
I am now twenty and he was thirty-two,
I was nowhere near ready and neither were you,
My mind in a spin,
I sure hope you're healthy in there,
As your life in this world will soon begin,
Mum is sorry from the start
    as I know I will get it sometimes wrong,
Wanting you to know now that is okay,
To have some days when it is not alright,
To have some days where it will be a fight,
My mum is Oma to you,
The epitome of a German lady for all to see,
She will help me look after you,
Gosh, what am I going to be?
I am going to be your Mummy,
Your Oma comes to all my appointments to do with you,
She says I am big but healthy,
How does a tummy get so huge?

My toes I cannot see,
I keep going for a frequent wee,
Oma will be the best for you,
Your bond will be like no other,
You will look after each other,
You see she has pain deep inside,
A story not mine to tell,
You will help mend that I see that now,
I will make sure you have fun,
Holidays and opportunities,
Not long now, my sweet baby, and you will be here,
Not going to lie, it is quite a joy but also a fear.

2020
Coronavirus

Sunshine beaming and crowds all out,
Many people listen and some will not,
Such trauma about without a doubt,
Restrictions will worsen, can you not see?
Think of other people and not that automatic rebel thought,
Some are life-threatening,
Boris, I believe is doing the best he can
    and meeting with our Queen,
We didn't know what was coming, give him a break,
All being human, mistakes we make,
Rainbows in all around,
Love to be found,
Some communities coming together,
Clapping for the medical staff,
Still managing to help a bit and having the odd laugh,
Unusual times yet kindness admits the fear,
Better times will come, they are near,
Cling on to hope and pray every day,
Take your faith and have it as your best friend,
Pray for the world to soon be on the mend,
Loss of lives and compassion we feel,
No idea when it will end,
Hang on in there, I am praying with many others,
My church is handing out supplies,
Still seeing those people smile,

I believe in this country and always will,
I believe in world peace and that starts with our community,
Let's be here for everyone,
Thank you to all the key workers from schools to care homes,
Hospitals, of course, and police and all services to see,
Thank you for being there,
Thank you for your inner care.

1990

PREGNANCY

Waddling around, getting ready for you,
You have a daddy excited to call you princess,
You have a big sister, who will be nearly three,
She cannot believe there is a baby inside me,
We told her you will come out of my belly button,
Why do we do that? You have to laugh,
Daddy has bought you a giant giraffe,
I say I will raise you both the same,
How can that be?
My own needs were different back to see,
I promise fun and as many holidays as I can,
I promise also I will sometimes get it wrong,
I promise I will raise you to say it will be alright in the end,
I promise I will be there at every difficult bend,
My head is often a mess,
I am sorry about all the times you may think 'Mother, honestly',
Loving you oooodles has already begun,
Daddy and I will always love you shnookleplum,
Reach for the stars,
Ignore the world if it says no,
Be you and make sure you do it your way so you grow,

Your daddy can sing you know?
He is looking forward to that lullaby,
Nanny cannot believe her baby will be a dad,
She is his rock and where he goes when he is sad,
Now, I do not have it all together that is for sure,
Just remember you are wanted and loved, for that is no cure,
Your life is what you want it to be,
Ignore the others and be where you want to be,
Leap, jump and sing for eternity.

MAY 2021
SMILING

Smiling alone or with everyone,
Living in the past cannot be done,
I have finally learnt the lessons I needed to learn,
Granted, it took me a long time and I am still learning,
Healing is what I need to do,
So, I can bless others along the way,
Faith is something that got me through,
God has promises that are really true,
I have got this with a grateful thank you,
Handling people with a better attitude,
Finally having a little grace,
Accepting I will always get some things wrong,
Accepting I will sometimes feel I do not belong,
Analyzing myself for a reflection to see,
That is ok to not always be me,
Knowing now I can handle things differently,
I do not need to be around that drink,
I do not need to be on edge with those people to sink,
To all the people I cannot say I am sorry and put the wrong right,
I will do good things in your name,
If I have wronged you, please get in touch,
I love all people and want to mend what is right,
I do not want to have that fight,
If I can put it right instead,
Also, help the homeless be fed,

Let's see the good in every day,
Ask God, may I see what you want me to see,
Ask to be who He wants you to be,
I know I will never be without sin,
Yet it seems serving others is what it's about,
Whenever I battle or hear myself shout,
I bless someone and it all goes away,
Then I am ready to face a fresh new day.

Sorry Again

Being sorry again,
Yup, that is me,
Letting him go,
Moving again,
Not wanting to show,
Will I ever stay and not run?
Do I even belong here? I fear not,
Something is wrong, I cannot seem to get it right,
I just have to go hug a tree,
Then I am alright inside me,
I am little bits of everyone I meet,
Some definitely I do not want to be,
Some I stay clear of day and night,
Some are dear souls and some give me a fright,
Doors knocking and I keep going in,
Damn it, slam it shut and say no way,
So, peace can start to have a place,
Shedding yet another tear,
Especially as not believed this time,
Why does it make me go out of my mind?
This adult thing, I wanted to be here,
Now wishing to be a child again,
Now wishing to know what I didn't know then.

1979
CLASS

English and Religious education classes,
Simply the best for me,
Expressing on paper, writing away,
My head is full of junk,
Getting it all out,
Who can I grab to talk it through, not you or him,
    or her over there,
English and R.E do listen you see,
Two women who are definitely in the right jobs,
They hear me a little and say it will all be okay,
Because of these two, I face another day,
Bullying girls, the compass in my side,
Cycling so fast I hit the wall,
Laughing at me when I had the fall,
Chewing gum in my long blonde hair,
Every day is a pain in the rear,
Will it end? Can I not stay at home?
That skiing trip they made me go on,
Rana couldn't come, I went all alone,
You girls know what you did to me,
Oh, skiing instructor, you should be ashamed,
The barman who took my big note and gave me no change,
Teachers drinking and too shy to ask,
An awful time, when will it end?
Back to school,
Face another day,
Something must be better than this,
This simply takes the piss.

Christian Music

No matter what is going on in my life,
The hymns settle inside my brain,
Close your eyes,
Listen to the song,
Reading the lyrics in between,
What would I do without you?
Where would I be?
Nope, not going there,
A beautiful day,
Lord, thank you for believing in me,
I am certainly on a journey and feeling your glow,
You're real and I just want others to know,
If you can forgive me,
I need them to know you'll meet them wherever they are,
Some are near and some are far,
Sometimes in the journey, people get removed,
Trust the process,
The right people catch you up,
God heard the conversation that you did not,
Your back he absolutely has got,
Takes time and you forever learn,
Reactions will change for a peaceful pause,
You'll find a root way with a great cause,
Prayer is so powerful at night,
Grateful for getting you through that day,
Trust in tomorrow and learn from before,
Remember opportunities are at each door,

Put the music on, whether a good or negative day,
Just listen and smooth it all away,
Looking back and seeing how far you have come,
Music does this,
Reminds you how it all began,
No amount of gold can take this place,
Worship or simply done in prayer,
That time alone or in Church,
What a beautiful plan he has for you,
Yes, it really is true.

May 2021
Woods

Listening to all the sounds around me,
Trees that have been here a mighty long time,
Pausing in the moment, in this life of mine,
Having goals and peace,
Having faith is the real key for me,
I get it finally,
Looking within,
Happiness is in all of us,
Within our minds and our souls,
Compassion for everything,
Not just people,
Gratitude for the woods right here,
The sound of them in the wind,
If they could tell their story,
Life is being more quiet and listening,
Observing behaviour and remembering the bigger picture,
Seeing a red flag for safety,
Yet, the inner love for them is there,
Showing you care,
So many think they are not good enough,
I was one and it is tough,
Telling the world, it is not possessions to have,
Gratitude for what you already own,
Not having another loan,
Seeing something simple has made my day.

Colour Red,

Shines bright,
Looks beautiful and all together,
Christian reasons also,
Never changing,
Not mistaking,
My second favourite colour,
Red scarf on a person,
Is so beautiful,
Man, woman or child or a neckerchief on a hound,
Red makes it glorious all around,
Positivity in it I see,
For all things, red brings me a smile,
Even if a sad memory, remember they're good,
So much in life can be misunderstood.

WAKING UP IN MAY

Stretching with the sun rising,
Not everyone is ready to see,
Dogs barking and children playing outside,
Birds tweeting beautiful songs,
Sitting on the patio for your first hot drink of a wonderful day,
How beautiful is the month of May,
All bulbs coming into flower,
People with a spring in their step,
Don't save the dress for a special day,
Every day is a miracle to be here,
Some don't have that good fortune and their life is cut short,
The past has now been,
The future is not guaranteed,
Plant that wonderful in-the-moment seed.

It Won't Come To You

Don't be shy,
Go and make a new friend,
Join that club,
Walk into that church,
Heal you and be on the mend,
If the first walk-in is not for you, try another one,
The battle is yours to be won,
Be around those who want you to be well,
Who support you to move forward and not dwell,
Whatever you class as positivity for your home,
Maybe for you, it's a huge smiling gnome,
De-clutter your home and give something away,
I promise you will feel good,
That person will one day do the same,
Then slowly it's the pass-the-happiness forward game,
Buy someone a cup of tea,
Have a ball of knitting on your knee,
Grab life with both hands,
Fold them together and say thank you,
Opportunities arise each day,
Age does not matter, it's never too late,
Ponder happily on the bench by the gate,
We are rich without wealth,
Reactions on how we view life and health.

WHAT I DO

Soaring waves crashing down,
She is leaving me,
Where has she gone?
Sickness has overtaken her mind,
I can touch her fingers, can she feel mine?
Deepened hurt,
Pacing, kicking up the garden dirt,
Dealing with all wrong,
Human nature won't allow me to leave it alone,
What do I do? How do I feel?
This soon will pass I know,
So-called friends of hers making that call,
Sitting in the hospital bed,
Looking at the sheet the doctor wrote,
Doctor says she should not be in bed,
Tears rolling down her face,
Hospital room, full of stale alcohol smell,
Illegally driven car outside,
Not knowing how to deal,
No Mum or Dad to turn to for advice,
Seeing you in there I can,
Life is totally unfair,
Knowing you do not know how to get out of your muddle,
Guessing you have not learnt what you need yet,
That is my hopeful bet,
Tired and red-eyed myself, my body is not coping anymore.

Need a fresh look at this and give it to prayer,
Your getting sick totally broke my heart,
Wishing it could have been me,
No one is at fault here,
What do I do?
No book of instructions here,
Please do not leave me I fear,
Third-party messages,
These people are not for you,
When you are ready let us draw closer to heal that pain,
How do I respond?
Boundary breaking,
There is a glimpse of you,
Holding on to that light,
Now for me, I have to draw back in fright,
Strength is weakening,
More than any trauma before,
When I lost my mum, I was nearly done,
Now, this is a whole new dimension,
Nobody knows how to help me deal,
Your whole mind has been torn,
Where did you go?
Such a speedy dip to show,
When you're working and with the encouraging crowd,
Such a different spirit,
I know it is not done on merit,
Stuck in the annoying rut,
Just in two years your world and choices have changed,
Scars are there,
Courage and strength you need like never before,
I will love you forever more.

Trust Yourself

Sun cap on and shady eyes,
Listening to your all-so-frequent lies,
When someone shows you who they are,
Have peace with it all, forgive, but keep them afar,
Surround yourself with whatever your faith may be,
No, it isn't selfish to take a wide berth,
God removes some people forever and some for a while,
Seasons differ, have faith,
Toxicity is not the way,
Prayer and good ears will get you through,
Believe in yourself,
Like God believes in you,
Be careful with the choices you act on and do,
We can always slip and be the same,
Sometimes it is praying daily for that very name.

LIFE

Close your eyes,
Dream big,
Live clean,
Limit alcohol and party life,
Limit all the chaos and strife,
Stand still and breathe, let the air into your lungs,
Take some photos,
Enjoy that stroll,
Watch the butterflies,
Read God's promises out loud,
Be you if you are in the crowd,
Open the window for the breeze,
Little giggles amongst the life tease,
Join the library,
So much to do,
Rat racing is not for humans to join,
Collections maybe for the rare coin,
Stamps may be your thing,
Avoiding the dangers of wine and the need for greed.

Written by my eldest Granddaughter who was 11 at the time

It is what it is,
Boris getting sick wasn't nice to hear,
Has he even got time with his new baby I fear,
I don't want his job at all,
All people saying this and that,
When do we actually have the facts,
Why did so many take all the toilet rolls,
What about those in need?
So many had unusual greed,
I did like the wildlife, more was around,
Even the odd deer or fox to be found,
No smelly cars either and fewer on the road,
No huge lorry with his heavy load,
My brother learnt to ride his bike,
I'm secretly proud of him,
Nanny missed church singing a hymn,
And Mum gave up smoking,
That's worth more than a diamond ring,
So as we open now,
Let's be nice and listen to the rules,
Remember the good of it and not be a fool.

CLIFF RICHARD

Loving you since I was eleven,
Kissed my poster of you on the way to school,
Headphones of an evening to your voice,
Coming alive and wanting to rejoice,
Thank you for so many years of simply being you,
Your music, clean living, an inspiration to see,
Now in my fifties, look back on growing up with you,
Whether I did not make the grade,
Being bullied was also tough,
Raging hormones especially rough,
Your smile all around my room and music
     playing in my ear,
Somehow took away life's real fear,
Mum taking me to my first concert,
Many more to come,
So many there, enjoying having fun.

Take The Good

Take the good, not the bad,
Take the joy, not the sad,
Feel the emotion and let it be,
Really feel it inside to see,
Then let it go and do not live there,
Whatever went wrong is a lesson, not life guilt,
Stepping stones for your life to be built,
Breathe in and exhale and enjoy the gap silence,
We all make mistakes,
Every one of us falls,
Now, grasp the daily opportunity to have it all,
Pain does not always go away,
So, make room for it and still find a way,
You will soon see the positive stories to be told,
You will soon see that a good life is to unfold,
Surround yourself with where you want to be,
Surround yourself and continue to see,
You are the author, so write your new chapter
    that is to begin,
Beautiful moments become amazing memories to win.

SARAH

We met in high school,
We probably found a way to break a rule or two,
Truant once or twice,
Eating my mum's angel delight,
Sharing our experiences as we grew,
Some things were amazing and we had no clue,
You have grown into a wonderful woman, Mum and friend,
You many a time have helped me on the mend,
Beautiful and kind children, they sure are like you,
Miles apart we are seeing each other this summer,
Coffee shops and to the stables to see Jenny ride,
With you, I never need to hide,
Heartfelt catch-ups,
Putting the world to right,
Being with you is never a struggle, it is a loving bright,
Precious times I recall,
Look at us now,
Settled and happy to call our own,
Fully adult and fully grown,
Thank you for standing by my side,
Through thick and thin,
You would say it will be okay,
Tomorrow is another new day,
I am loving life now,
My faith and family have a say,
Thank you, my friend,
Pure precious to the end.

Memory Loss They Say

Back and forth to the consultant man,
Saying my brain is working differently,
When I see what you can't see,
When I'm wanting to be just me,
In a world full of noise,
Overwhelming for some to understand,
Trying to have life's upper hand,
Climbing back into my home,
Closing the door,
My world is all I know,
Vulnerable category they say,
To be careful in my day-to-day,
Always wanting to live alone,
In my fifties,
In my Zone,
Standing on my own two feet,
Though, wandering away from the appointment seat,
In my own little glare,
Not always being very aware.

Remember To Walk Away

Walking away before your angry face shows all around,
No words said that can't be taken back,
Turning to say no more,
Pain cannot torture like before,
Wisdom setting in,
Compassion deep within,
There is always a bigger picture if we choose to see,
Most people want health and happiness, including you and me,
Reaching a point, where we turn to walk away,
Let's approach this conversation another day,
We all feel pain and hurt deep down,
I don't want to make it any worse,
I don't feel the need to curse,
No blame here, so let's get on with the rest of today,
Tomorrow we can rationally have our say.

Grandchildren

Not known a love like it, for all five,
They make my heart beat faster and bring me alive,
How is life in your world? I ask,
Then listen to such inspiring answers from different ages,
Growing up fast, all at different stages,
Thirteen down to four years old,
All very different, more precious as they unfold,
We can learn so much from their points of view,
No need to act wiser or confused,
Holding their hand, which is open for me,
Being a nanny is a huge responsibility,
One at a time to come and stay over,
Cooking, crafts with some swimming and a laugh,
Watching them deal with everything at school,
Hearing stories that can be so cruel,
Another time belly laughing until we cry,
Painting pebbles and baking while they dry,
Sometimes the best thing I can do,
Praying for each child to fully know you.

Outside and Breathe

Living in a world of challenges,
Finding it hard to keep on top,
All that rain, poor people and animals,
Will the farmers lose their crops?
Fires in Australia, there must be great fear,
Sometimes my prayers aren't always clear,
Lord be with each disaster,
Let them know you are right here,
Unable to comprehend what they are going through,
We see it all through the news channel view,
Wanting them to know that they are not alone,
It's not like we can randomly pick up their phone,
Power in our prayers for those suffering right now,
Power in our prayers for the ones in need of shelter and food,
Power in prayers to lift people's low moods,
World disasters and confusion are everywhere,
Governments fighting each other and not part of a team,
Making it difficult for us to understand what they mean,
World peace starts with you and me,
Compassion for everyone to see.

Each Day At A Time

Step by step and then pause to break,
Silence amidst the thinking really counts,
Snowball play,
Seeing if the neighbour is okay,
Quiet time reading a book,
Prayer time going through a list,
Never driving through a mist,
Mailing angels in the snow,
Watching your children fully grow,
Roasted chestnuts and marshmallows,
Walking over the park,
Not being alone out in the dark,
Christmas carols and Easter real-time,
Watching the farmer spread the lime,
Wondering how to cope when it's a bit overwhelming,
Joining a choir to have a sing,
Sometimes bed or a Pajama Day,
Sometimes, some time on your own,
Especially if in a crowd you feel alone,
Being an encouragement to others, including myself,
Not everyone's brain works in the same way,
Some have to work hard to get up every day,
Step by step and pause in between,
Each day at a time,
Let everyone grow in their own way,
Little bits of Progress keep negativity at bay.

Available worldwide from Amazon and all good bookstores

www.mtp.agency

www.facebook.com/mtp.agency

@mtp_agency

Milton Keynes UK
Ingram Content Group UK Ltd.
UKHW020035211023
431026UK00011B/196